A GW

A GWYNEDD SYMPHONY

Tony Conran

commissioned by Gwynedd
County Council, 1996

1996

GOMER

First Impression—1999

ISBN 1 85902 579 X

© Tony Conran

Tony Conran has asserted his right under the Copyright, Designs and
Patents Act, 1988, to be identified as Author of this Work.

This book is published with the support of the
Arts Council of Wales.

Printed in Wales by
Gomer Press, Llandysul, Ceredigion

O brightening glance,
How can we know the dancer from the dance?

W. B. Yeats

FERNS BY LLYN CLYD

Cantref of Arfon

1

I've a propensity for not
Climbing mountains. Y Garn –
Between the higgledy-piggledy
Block scree of Idwal
(The Devil's Kitchen
Where every boulder's a house
Speciality) and
The blue slate of Elidir's
Remorseless spoiltips
Whitening with lichen. Y Garn –
Even now,
The peak eluded me.

                    I was seduced.

Suddenly, in my ungainly scrambling
I heard
Like a butler
The raven cough . . .

And there –

A new Earth, was it? An untrodden
Sunlight without bloodstains
Clouding it, gravel and tarn
Like hope, glistening.

                    I know now
Why I'd climb mountains, if I did.

The triangles point down, ride
The grey silences: beech ferns
In a cavalcade, wind
Through bank and cleft
Boulder, the neat cloaks
Draping their saddles.

Hard fern, a nest
Of snipers, watching
With rifles tall
And at ease –
In the miniature heath
Sit up like hares.

Sweet mountain fern, lemon
And white – long
Regiments bonneted
In shuttlecocks,
Stocked, narrow-throated
Men o' the line.

And between them, everywhere,
The clubmosses kneel,
Scale-coated sappers
From that first
Silurian putsch
Greening the dry.

It's a tattoo
For the mesozoic.

Look close, you'll see
A brontosaurus
Mouse-size, peep between them . . .
An ancient ordnance
(Listen!) readies for battle
To a bronze trumpet's bray

3

Did the death of the dinosaurs
Mean nothing
Here? Whatever
Clash of planets,
Burst of supernova,
Ice Age, busted them,

This lake, Llyn Clyd,
Curled up, survived . . .

But no, look how young
These ferns
Crowd the balconies!
They're kids like Juliet,
Young opportunists
In love. The next cold

Will weed them. Like goldcrests
A pretty plumage
Will draggle the stone.
Theirs is no survival
Against time, but
Every year's holocaust.

Anyway, nothing in these
Glaciated hills
Is old. A few thousand
Years marks the
Utmost genealogy,
Hereabouts, of life.

There are places, Tenerife,
Madeira, even Southern England,
Where life's coeval

With the rock. Deaths
Leapfrog each other, back
To the land's origin.

Not here. A mile-high chisel of ice
Erased all recent death.
Nothing's continuous
With what swam or sank
In this mudstone. Life-wise,
Gwynedd's a new land.

4

. . . And then the melt-down.
Crashing, grinding,
Scooping a spoonful

Of chopped rock
Out of this corrie, the lip
And the dark lake.

The whole land scoured –
Not a draggle of grass,
Not a lichen.

Clinical, save for
Clattering streams
At the first rain.

And then, refugees,
Nomads, sporelings
Out for a quick buck.

Gipsy and low-caste
Soilmakers hitched
On the upwind.

A new Earth, then? Sunlight
Without bloodstains
Clouding it, gravel and tarn
Like hope, glistening?

                    Yes,
At this corrie of comfort
I can feel Gwynedd
Like a Klondyke hitching me
Upwind to gold –
A new country,
Settler's home.

In the untrodden light
Come travellers
– Pilgrims or refugees.

The young ferns
Crowd their balconies.
At the next cold
Opportunists
Draggle the heart.

Refugee camp –
Or a quality of light
Drawing us inward . . .
Which is it?

Too late for the peak

And to the braying of a trumpet
I stumble down again
The loose stones
Of my path.

WINTER AT LLANDDWYN

The ruined shrine of Dwynwen
patron saint of lovers

Cantref of Rhosyr

1

Not to dance. To sit it out
In the storm, in the level sunlight
All winter, deciduous.

With wings pegged on the line
Cormorants hang like scarecrows.
The islands are so near.

The gulls' clattering quarrel
Reaches downwind
In a high melancholy wail.

It empties the air,
This winter calm.
There's nothing to think.

Will the prelude
Break on a downbeat,
A crescendo of excitement?

The curtain of time
Stays shut, curls
Only at the edge, like ripples.

Will the cold islands
Reveal themselves
A scena, or pas de deux?

2

A girl here. A man. An expectation.
It was as if in the gentle savagery of love
They danced, hardly touching –

Even a kiss broke the concentration
Of their waiting, even a reaching hand
Startled in a rush of wings.

In the rhyme of bodies, alliterations
Of moving together, mirrorings –
An inseparable separation.

Time was created in the first moments
When their eyes met. Like a dance
In its performance, nothing

Before that counted. Prehistory
Only inferred in the quality
Of gesture, a fossil acquaintance.

3

But then, she broke it.

– Why?

– There are answers, of course.
Father opposed to it, a dynasty
To be thought of . . . Or was it
A sudden, inexplicable
Failure of belief, an injury
Like a finger cut off
To a fiddler?

– Or did he overreach himself
In some way, and offend her?

– She showed no anger.

– He did, though.

– She had betrayed him?

– Betrayed the two of them. He saw her
Choose to make nothingness
Of what they'd been.
Very well, his body would show her –
Tell her how nothingness felt. He forced her,
Pulled her down, stripped her . . .

– Didn't she cry out?

– He left her, in the contempt he felt for her
A day and a night. She was unclean –
Her father tried to hide her
But there was nowhere left,
Nowhere beyond the mirroring.

– It was terrible for her.

– But he was destroyed by it,
Maddened by the ice
That scooped life out of him.
He would have starved . . .

4

It was then God chose her,
Then, or at the beginning
Of the world, in the nothingness.

It is said that an Angel came
With a new mirroring. He showed her
Maelon, her lover, frozen in the ice.

God gave her three wishes . . .

This winter calm
Empties the air.
There's nothing to think.

Though in the pool
Configurations of fishes
Prophesy (or lovers say they do)

And birds on the islands
Live out their natural
Appetitive hysterias –

The clipped sarcasm of gulls,
The cormorants –
Seals roll on their backs and sing . . .

Yet God chooses
In the nothingness
Before the curtain's drawn

Where the dancers from the green room
Wait to cross into time
As their eyes meet his

And there's nothing to think
But the dance
And the empty light.

THE RHIWLEDYN MASS OF BLESSED WILLIAM DAI

priest and martyr
executed Biwmares, 1593

Cwmwd of Creuddyn in the
Cantref of Rhos

1

I shall go to God's altar,
To God who gives my youth joy . . .

Toehold to toehold,
Impetuous, only seeing
The rock I could reach,
I climbed the cliff.

Send out your light and truth.
They bring me to your holy hill.

Suddenly I looked down –
Froze, terrified
Against white stone.
The hanging world was spinning.

You being my strength, God,
Why do you rubbish me?

Now I could not look.
I was locked like cramp –
Shipwreck of silence
Through those long minutes.

Judge him, God. Plead his cause.
From treachery save him!

That child on the cliff –
The white rockface
On the Little Orme
Scrauped by his heartbeats –

As he goes to God's altar,
To God who gives joy.

2

The tragic actor waits his cue.
Unworthiness
Duns him like creditors.
Hypocrite, two-faced –

How is he fit to be king?
To have the plum part,
The suffering hero?
To offer body and blood?

In the apron he bends.
One fist pummels his rib.
He whispers, calls out
In the wavelength of the holy.

'Ho,' he cries, 'theatre people,
All who've ever acted
On this tump of the skull,
I confess to you,

And to you, who play chorus,
Who wait in the wings,
Who are audience,
I confess . . .'

And we hear him out.
Our lips move in absolution
And we answer, 'Sir,' we say,
'The roles are greater than we know.'

We confess to the company
And to him, our unfitness
To be at that treachery
And that breaking of bread.

3

And now he moves out onto the hill.
He remembers the cave,*
The printshop
And the whirring of the press.

How the pages slammed down,
Blackmarketed
For the first time, Welsh
In a printed book!

Y Drych Cristianogol –
Mirror in the green room,
The cave on Rhiwledyn
Where they set up the Type.

---

* After William Dai (or Davies) returned to Wales as a priest he and other
Catholics founded a secret press in a cave on Rhiwledyn (the Little Orme)
and produced the first book ever to be printed in Wales: *Y Drych
Cristianogol*, 'The Christian Mirror.'

4

He goes into the high place.
He recites his entrance.
And we crowd round him,
The tragic chorus dance.

Invoking the god
A ninefold, ancient, untranslated cry:
'Kyrie, have mercy,
Kyrie eleison.'

By a simple re-location of stance
And a renewal of greetings
Without change of mask
Or disrobing,

He becomes messenger,
Storyteller,
Remembrancer
Of a holy people.

He announces the themes.
He journeys, he is oracle.
He tells the beginning
Of the vortex of the Word.

5

A second time the chorus dances.
Hurrying feet affirm what we know –
God's oneness, the carpenter,
The only begotten . . .

We're replying to the messenger
With what he knows and we know,
Or what he thinks he knows
And what we think we believe.

Amen. Et vitam venturi saeculi.
The life of the world
Venturing, so be it,
Into our future. Into our dying.

The ministry of the word,
The printing press
In the hill Rhiwledyn,
Scattered to the sea and wind.

6

Till the dance is done with, the coded
Footfall of narrative silenced
And the claim to resurrection
Laid

The actor sits, recollecting himself.
Now he rises, greets the people.
Rides, as Son of Man,
To sacrifice.

Holding the hostage of time,
The bread, the immaculate wafer,
Offers it for himself, for those
Who play chorus,

Who wait in the wings,
Who are audience . . .

His gaze widens. To Dinerth
Over the saltmarsh,
East to his own home,
Croes-yn-Eirias:

For maids and farm labourers
Of Uwch Dulas, his cwmwd,
For wives and tradesfolk,
He offers it,

For the lost parishes of Creuddyn –
Llangystennin, Llanrhos, and high
On the table of the Orme,
Llandudno.

Westward to Seiriol's island,
Penmon, and his place of death . . .

And again his thought widens. Gwilym
From a family of harpers,
Telynorion, gives hostage
For them –

For cyweirdant and tyniad,
For variety of plucking,
For the twenty-four measures
Caniad and gosteg –

Being part of the mirroring
Of God's love
In the order of Wales,
Y Drych Cristianogol –

All the rough and tumble
Of minstrels, and the prosody
Free and intricate
As the growth of an oak.

It's down on its uppers, that Wales!
The patrons gone whoring
Like the newfangled bishops
After strange gods . . .

But wider, wider, for all Gwynedd,
For Britain, Christendom
And everywhere, men and women,
He offers the host. The hostage of time.

7

It is Passover in the upper room.
The president of the supper
Shows us viands,
Each with its story.

The chorus like a young child
Is expected to ask
'What's this? Why that?
Can I drink it?'

In riddling stichomythía
As each line parries the last
We winkle him out of his secrets,
Rabboni, at the feast.

8

The actor turns from us.
The back of his head is a mask
Through which he speaks
Persona Christi, Christ's impersonator.

In the land of the Trinity
He raises his voice.
In the mead hall of the noble
The reacaire spreads his arms.

The atceiniad begins his boast.
The brag of God's doings
From the beginning of the world . . .

This rhapsode has his lines by heart.
He does not stumble
Nor his voice crack at the rhyme.
The cynghanedd is sweet.

'For the man,' says he, 'in whom our eyes
Once looked at visible Godhead,
Takes us now in invisible love
Through the tomb, through the opening.

We crowd to touch him,
To be healed, to be accepted.
God looks at himself in this man
And sees us. We are one.

The six-winged seraphs
Who brought fire to the lips –
They are artists, they are poets
Of the loveliness of God.

We must sing their song –
Dance at the furnace
Where stars are forged
Like the cherubs of his thought . . .'

A third time, therefore,
The chorus dances
To the glory, the holy one
Of Sabaoth.

'Hosanna on high!
He is blest who comes
In God's name.
Hosanna!'

And in the silence then, the human actor
Resumes his boast.
His fingers feel the scarring nails
As he touches the bread.

Judas is slipping away into the darkness.
There's a kiss at the end of it
And a rope on a tree
With a friend's dead weight.

His fingers reach for the bread.
'This is my body,'
And for the wine,
'This is my blood.'

RAM

Cwmwd of Ardudwy

As if he remembered something
He looks up from the grass
And chooses.

Perhaps he'd already chosen.
The ewe was ten yards away.
Was she tempting him?

One of those progressions
Half a walk,
Half a dance –

Like an Apprentice Boy
With the lambeg
Beating for King William –

But milder than that,
A real march of love
No haste or aggression.

Deliberately he trots high
Like a horse reined in
– Dangos ei bedolau mae o –

Shows off his shoes,
The two-toed delicacy
Almost like a gazelle.

Rhythmically, as he walks,
The long head with its twin
Spirals of grey horn

Deliberately nods.
Like a courtier to Queen Anne
Bows down, bows down.

His Roman nose nearly touches the ground
As he nods his horn,
As he honours the ewe.

He could almost be carrying a banner,
A cross in the crook of his elbow
Like the Lamb of God.

Five or six times he bows
As he walks those ten yards
Between two kinds of time.

He reaches the chosen one
And slows himself, slews round
Till he breathes in her ear.

Very gently, he lifts one foot,
His knee caresses her.
They wait together.

It seems like centuries.
Love's tide must turn
In the silence.

From the ebb of creation
To its flood
Two or three minutes,

Two or three millenia
His knee measures
Against her flank.

He has her attention.
And now I notice
The twig trailing his belly.

He turns round, sniffs her rump.
There's sensuality now.
Time's clicking back into place.

But the never-never air
Of autumn
In this dry pasture by the sea

Still haunts his mounting of her.
Ambiguous time
Suffuses for a while yet

His flesh – before he leaves her
As if suddenly remembering
Grass . . . the necessity of grass.

PILGRIMAGE

A myfi a fum naw mis haiach
yng nghroth Ceridwen y wrach
Taliesin

(And I was indeed nine months
in the womb of Ceridwen the hag)

1

Three children
Herding sheep
In Santorém.

'I am the Rosary –
Lady of Ave
Our father
And gloria.'

She came to them
One spring day
Lady of Ave
Our father
And gloria –
They found her with their sheep
By Fátima
In Santorém.*

* On May 13 1917 and each subsequent month until October, three peasant
children of Fátima in the district of Santorém in Portugal had a vision of one
who called herself the Lady of the Rosary. The Roman Catholic Church in
Bala was the first church outside Fátima itself to be dedicated to Our Lady of
Fátima.

A week of months,
Lady of Ave
Our father
And gloria –
God's mother
Shepherded her sheep with them
By Fátima
In Santorém.

2

Three college friends
– He, she and I –
He gay, she
In love with him
And I halfway
In love with her –

Three friends
For his degree –
From a winter of working,
April with 'shoures soote'
Had pierced with shoots
The droughty soul

And wended he, she, I
On pilgrimage
To a far hallows . . .
Bala, first ever
Shrine of Fátima,
To pray.

It took us nine hours.

Stopping in Ogwen, climbers
Booted and breeched,
In ramshackle Austins
Freighted us in.

Not yet a Catholic, I went
Trudging between wet walls –
Capel Curig and the bullocks
Inquisitive at us,

Hardly a car in sight –
Took us nine hours.

In Betws y Coed, Betws of the trees,
The unrolling bright ferns
Starring the dark,
We sang our Angelus.

Raggedly we sang –
Took us nine hours.

Not yet a Catholic, I came
At sunset, into the wide Bala street –
Five minutes to pray
Till the shrine was locked.

Five tired minutes
Took us nine hours.

4

We knew so little.
Three children, too late
Arriving for a party.

Even of each other, knowledge
Was emulsified
All white, like milk.

She knew more. Her sharp love
Had separated
The curds and whey –

Light could reach through
And it frightened her,
Twinkled with sadness.

He knew one thing. It loomed
Over him, a shadow
Like style, farce, self-absorption.

I knew nothing. Like the universe
In the first ten seconds
Opaque to radiation.

Emulsified; but feeling
The deep drift
Crowd me to this hag's cauldron,

Bala, by Llyn Tegid,
Where it boiled and spat at me
Five tired minutes

And perhaps it was then
I put my divining finger in my mouth
To suck off the scald

And I heard language
Of love and grief
Colour the whiteness

Before I ran to my changes,
Hare, fish, bird,
Grain of wheat

And the hag after me,
Greyhound, otterbitch, falcon . . .
Black, scratching hen.

SENDING A HARRIER TO LLANEILIAN

I.M. Bedwyr Lewis Jones,
Professor of Welsh at Bangor

Cantref of Cemaes

1

Low over the rough pasture, dark harrier,
As if you'd lost a key
You search dank ground.

Flap slowly upwind, tread air . . .
You grip your wings
Like a divining rod.

Their shallow V dips
As you peer
Into reed and rush.

Momentarily you hover, your white skirts
Swirling, turn
To focus on a vole.

Delicate, murderous hands
Prepare to drop . . .
Not this time, though!

A twitch of impatience – and the huge
Fingering wings
Shrug it off,

Flap to regain
Inertia . . .Your problems
Are those of scholarship,

The aeronautics of slowness
In a featureless
Terrain –

For a yard at a time, to read
With your magnifying eye
Black-letter of earth.

2

Hen harrier, as I watch you
The memory
Of Bedwyr
Flicks through the pages.

I've lost a key
From my ring –
A key to openhanded
Welshness,

A key to the hospitality
Of Tywyn and Nannau.
I've lost a scholar,
Vade mecum of learning.

A key to priest-lofts,
To glory-holes,
Civilization
In brown almanacs.

I've lost a protector.
A key to the wardship
Of Wales, a hearth
Open as day.

A key to compassion,
To justice.
A key to the validity
Of Bangor in the world.

3

Hawk, if you'd find that key
Where it hides
In the crevices
Of grass . . .

Imagine you, wandering
In search of it,
Migrating
To the good lands,

Beating west-nor'-west
Across the westerlies,
Climbing to trip thermals
On the Carneddi,

Till all the variety
Of Gwynedd
Lies twisted and knuckled
At the edge of your eyes.

There's the long scabbard
Of Menai,
Decorated
With dinghies.

You're a dragon now,
Rummaging Wales
For a home, a courage,
A hospitality . . .

A tower with a pyramid spire –

Llaneilian
Like a galleon embattled
Towing a coracle –

The cell of its saint.

4

Musics of the tongue,
Of plucked strings,
Of chiselled wood.

Tracery of words, phonemes, syllables.
Tracery of pitch, tone-lengths, rhythm.
Tracery of uprights, curves, vineleaves . . .

The carved rood-loft
Like all traditional things
Waits to be used.

It dominates the nave
Not for itself, but to service
A cross long ago gone –

To illuminate,
To emblaze with candles
The hanging God.

A loft for musicians –
Look, two are carved
Under the beams,

With flute (is it?) and bagpipe,
The wide chanter
Wrapped by his hands.

And though their lips breathe
And they finger the notes,
Their eyes stare out:

Two stolid angels
As they play, look through us
To an ecstasy

That would burn,
Would char our eyes
In the brightness of their dark.

5

Scholar, this is the place.
Fly, elbow your wings
Round the green enclosure.

The key's here
Surely, in this mediaeval yard
Where the graves

Of children and wives, poets and farmers,
– God's acre –
Go back a millenium

To the saint himself,
Eilian
And the ruined spring –

Surely you'll find it . . .
See there, by the wall
Is Bedwyr's rest.

No, nothing's here.
Neither key nor opening –
Nothing!

– Only inside the church, a grotesque
Jabbering death,
A man of bone

Painted on the rood-loft,
For the first time
Claims our acquaintance –

Memento mori
With a wink of an empty socket
And a whistle of dry wind.

MORRIS AT DWYGYFYLCHI

Cantref of Arllechwedd

1

The lanes lead onto a village,
Two or three shops, a pub on a stone stage.

Cars by the hedges are like huge fungi.
They sit lopsided as toadstools

And once a year dehisce melodeons,
Concertinas, fiddles, mandolines

That fly from the fruiting bodies like spores
And come to rest in corners by pub tables

With clogs, coats, scribbled programs,
Bells, boxes of tissues and a carry-cot.

A men's side would act roles, play at misrule –
Imitation yokels leapfrog chairs,

Talk seriously of ale. This side is mixed,
The encounter muted, hardly larger than life –

Eating our pie and chips under the gap
Till music sprouts sporelings and we caper.

2

But there's a savagery
About the remaindered worlds

That meet in the pub's forecourt
As the baldricks joggle on breasts

And the flowered mad-hatter hats
Hey in the gleaming air.

Dwygyfylchi – where two gaps meet –
Is a place of invasions

And fifty yards up, a different world . . .

3

Hillforts straddle the horizon.

Shepherds, raw-faced from the wind
Banter in guttural Welsh.

They've been here so long, they look native.

4

But sheep are invaders too.

Ordivician chiefs in their low war-wagons
Like Masai, counted in cows.

Until the eighteenth century
Round here was beef country.

'Orwig, lord of Gwynedd, giver of cattle . . .'

But even Orwig, who built the dry-stone cities,
Kraals that we call hillforts

– Even Orwig and his Welsh –
Invaded through the gaps

A dolmen-littered, alien land . . .
A folk that piled cairns, raised henges

And had (in their turn) invaded
Tundra,
Glaciers . . .

5

We trundle out our irreverent hornpipes

– 'Shepherds' Hey'
    'Lillibolero'
        'Not for Joe' –

And for the nonce
    Like Cotswold farm-hands,
        We clash sticks

Or in elaborate parody of our betters

Vaunt like cocks,
    Flirt hankies,
        Bow.

THE GARDENERS

Cwmwd of Eifionydd

1

It was as if I'd promised
Nineteen years ago, to come . . .
As if my lanky phantom
Ran with bag and potted plant
To a waiting bus in Bangor,
Tumbled before the bell rang
To my seat, smiled at giggling
Schoolkids, puffed, arranged my rig.

Bus after bus. And then striding
Uphill, after a dodgem ride
To Borth-y-Gêst, as sunset
Closed the Red Book and grew dun –
Between dark hill of bracken
And white wall, a bridle track,
And a door at last opened
To the stone steps down the slope.

My father in the hallway
Welcomes me, smiling. The call
Signals of claustrophobia
Touch nerves like a dentist's probe.
Nineteen years this December
He died. But despite that, when
I haunt him, I'm the phantom –
He's the too too solid man.

2

My mother takes the plant,
Coddles like a new pet
This seedling I'm giving her.
We both know she's ruthless –
'Didn't earn its space,' she'll say.
'Didn't give much joy.'

'Kept dying on me.
A plant's got to like you
Or there's no point . . .'

Our propagations differ.
My mother makes cuttings – exactly
Clones what she desires.

I grow from seeds, invite
Wilderness in –
Each of my gardens

A potential forest,
Chaos of death and maimed growth
Like a battlefield.

3

The screen flicks. It is morning.
My mother stands by the lawn.
Thinks, and her thought's the garden.
Her music this paradise yard,
Carrying with her from England
A high culture, a bright ring,
Visionary growth, artwork
In leaf, a way of the heart.

All over India, learning
How to cool crimson with fern,
How to train bourgainvillea
Scarlet to the upstairs sill.
Gold stamens of hibiscus
Prod from the corolla's disk,
Deep blue of jacaranda,
White jasmine scenting the hand . . .

She planted gardens, grieving
Always that she had to leave
Before the paint dried – early,
Too early, her leaves would curl
To someone else's guilty
Neglect, their waterless wilt.
'Takes ten years for a garden
To take shape. India was hard.'

Thrown out, and back in England,
She'd new bushes to make sing.
From the crisp leaf of beechwoods
Learn what frost and fog could teach.
A whole new medium: nurseries
To haunt, wrong labels to curse,
And the intellectual measure
Of the art, to learn afresh.

4

All through their courtship
Foxtrot, charleston, black bottom
Ordered the wilderness.

The floor would clear to watch them.
'His brains are all in his feet,'
Said Uncle Stan.

Elegance and control
Of a couple locked
In a perfected routine . . .

My father served her gardens
Like an engineer.
Embankments, irrigation

He navvied for her, his interest
Only to tidy a routine:
To dance: to perfect a lock.

5

Cut. And pan. Round my bedroom
And me there, bending my head
At the low cottage window
Buffetted all night by wind
Though now a Christmas brightness
Uncurtained, steadies the sight
As long fingers of shadow
Lie quiet on my white bed.

The massive view envelopes
My parents' house like a spell:
Estuary of two rivers,
Dunes, rocks, the green fugitive
Streaks of brightness on tideways;
Cormorant's coasting, gull's glide,
Harlech, and the mist lifting
From fortress and mountain rift.

This last garden was 'state of the art':
It answered to theory –
Critics and soothsayers of shrubbery.

Haworth Booth, thatcherite of gardens:
Least work, most flower-power:
An arithmetic like market forces.

Christopher Lloyd, for whom
Affection and excitement
Provide consensus.

Or quaintness still holding its own –
Marjory Fish, a cave
Of gems, a secrecy of treasure.

From all the high gardeners of Britain
Her plants had pedigree,
All the civilization of England.

(I once went with my mother to Bodnant.
The great Mr Puddle, archpriest,
Confessed her in conclave . . .)

'State of the art' . . . Except for one thing:
At tree level her garden
Did not exist

And therefore, was helpless –
Just petered out
Where the view took over.

I have always distrusted views – vistas
Like autobahns and Cathedrals
And the master-race.

A great view's so one-sided, you forget
You're part of it.
You survey it like an empire

– And it not merely leaves you defenceless
Against force-ten huricane,
Salt burn, or revolution;

It also destroys the art. It puts limits
To one's friendship with a place.
The garden just peters out.

For in the economy of gardens
The only salve against vistas
Are trees –

Pines, stunted oaks, junipers
Protect the scale,
Make you lookable at,

Part of the land.

THE BULLS

Cantref of Meirionydd

1

Come, Dun Cow of Einion,
Stray-horns, Speckle o' the lake,
And Dodin the polled,
Up, come home.

– Each phrase tongued like a trumpet,
An ullulation winding
Down from a high scream
In melismas like a scree.

Then silence. A new phrase begins.
A scream, a yodel
Breaking out between stones,
Tumbling like a mountain spring.

Silence. The naming of cows
In an early morning –
The old woman eerily
Crying them home.

And the silences filled
With the moans and confabulations
Of cattle,
Rumours of great bulls.

Whether in twentieth century Telemark
Or Meirionydd
This was how
She called them, the cattle of the Tylwyth Teg –

Dere di, Felen Einion,
Cyrn Cyfeiliorn, Braith y Llyn,
A'r Foel Dodin,
Codwch, dewch adre.

Each name a new song
Falling from silence.

2

Buzzard of Brithdir, speckled land,
Where legionaries
Traipsed the Fault,
You kill in the trees.

Buzzard of Cross Foxes, two doors
Open: to the east
Oerddrws the cold.
You kill in red fern.

Buzzard of Garthgynfawr, to the south
The long Fault, the door
Through Cadair Idris.
Kill in grey rock.

Buzzard, eagles are gone. The grey heads
Roosted by the river,
Fished Afon Clywedog.

Buzzard, dead wood of their eyries
Is swept from the crag.
Gold heads have mouldered.

Buzzard, you kill in their brightness.
Through the nibbled
Mountain, the Fault veers west.

Buzzard, lazily you wheel,
Short-arse, mewing
To the watershed, to the sudden trees.

3

And the bus rounds the corner, and there
Below us, Tal-y-llyn, the lake
And the twelve miles unwinding
To Tywyn, straight as light.

For a whole minute, the validity
Of that road is in question.
Rock has opened. Do we go,
Like dead warriors, down to far havens?

Every time I come, it's sunset.
The lake, the wide ravine
Shines white gold
With a soft lovingness. The Fault –

O felix culpa – drops to the west.
Nightingales are singing. Oh, where
In those fading miles
Is it rich to die?

And then the bus swerves south
To Corris Uchaf, dead quarries
And the normal, leftover
Tips of industrial Wales . . .

The vision of disappearances
Itself disappears. But the scars
Left in the consciousness
Like moraines, like private lakes,

Reach out to lapping seas,
Underwater cities
Of the mind, Cantre'r Gwaelod
And the drunken dykes.

4

It's a countryside where disappearances
Come easy. A flickering
Like a vortex of existence
Between there and not.

Appearances too. Ghosts
Of old quarrels erupt from trees
And in the bearded lake-fringes
Otherworld cattle while the light away

Till in the dusk, green
Fairy women call to them,
And the white cows, heavy with milk,
Red-eared, troop

To deep water and are gone.
Once, a farmer bought one
Or was given it, for favour
Or love-gift, no one knows –

She made him rich, that cow,
Her yellow cream, and the cheeses
He could curdle from it,
And the strong calves she brought him.

But then he thought, she's old,
She'll be unprofitable.
I'll fatten her while there's time.
The knife hung in his hand

But in the silence, the songs started,
The naming of the stray cow
And her calves . . .

Each phrase tongued like a trumpet,
An ullulation winding
Down from a high scream
In melismas like a scree.

– Come, Dun Cow of Einion,
Stray-horns, Speckle o' the lake,
And Dodin the polled,
Up, come home.

Silences filled
With the moans and confabulations
Of cattle,
Rumours of great bulls . . .

He was left herdless,
Without cream or cheese
Or calves, save for a black runt.
Prosperity was gone. Died poor.

5

Disappearances cluster like bees.
Castell y Bere
Lies low on its mound.

No, it was here, not Cilmeri,
Not by the Irfon at Builth,
Wales drained like brown blood into peat.

The last bull-protector of Britain,
The last Princeps Gwaliae
Defended his corner. Fled.

Feckless Dafydd in the April storm
Took to his heels
As the curtain tumbled,

As the stage curtain collapsed.

6

What were they then, those cattle of the lakes
Huge white oxen with red ears
You could never keep?

I have seen Welsh blacks on the morfa at Harlech
Among the two rivers
Stand pooled in a dream of water –

All day, like toys in a window, stand
In the wader-pecked busyness
Of the shore, in the crowding tides.

I suppose wild cattle shared in that,
And from the scrubland would file down
To paddle in the shallow ends of lakes.

Wild bulls, the aurochs, six foot high
At the withers, tall as a man
And twice as long, with their cows

Like huge red antelope of the woods –
To rest their draggled legs
In the trout waters.

A folk memory of aurochs? The greed
Of a mountain farmer
For all that cow-flesh and imagined milk?

But why white? why dun, speckle
Or yellow?
Why Dodin the polled?

Aurochs were black or dark,
And their cows red brown,
Their horns high.

But were there perhaps, in those days
Before the oaks were chopped,
Feral cattle, as there are goats and ponies? –

Remains of Roman herds, white oxen
For beef or haulage:
Latium, like China, had no dairy habits –

The overflowing milk
Mere fairy-gold
For a rainbow's end.

Dere di, Felyn, Tarw gwanwyn,
Gwinau Gwylwylyd, a Thonllwyd,
A Brych, tarw Maelgwn
Codwch, dewch adre.

Bulls of the legions, in my lord's parks
Collected from the open woods like deer,
Chillingham, Vaynol –

Good for nothing now but to be wild,
Or remind us, like a zoo,
Of the bull-phantoms of Britain –

Come, Dun Bull, Pale Bull o' springtime,
Brown Puckerthroat, old Greyskin,
And Speckle, Maelgwn's bull –
Up, come home!

The bulls of sovereignty
Shall they come back to us,
Wild phantoms of Wales?

And the tall cows, shall they
By the lakes
Calve white, with perked red ears?

OLD MAN PLANTING CROCUS

for Maia

Maenol of Bangor

Room, room, for our mystery,
I gasp, give room!
The dog and I, motley
Like a puppet show
On a stone tomb.

My neck hangs wry,
My hands clatter.
I kneel precariously –
In the earth
Dibble and scatter.

Amid roots of wet grass
Push the thin trowel,
Twist a cigar out of soil –
Room for a grin
In a weather of scowl.

They are late to put in.
Each corm shows bud
Like a golden beak –
A promise of wings
In a wintry wood.

Push them into the hole,
Death's dry chaff
And the white flesh of the corm.
Room, room, for the newborn,
I gasp.

My crocus girl, mummers
– The dog and I –
Bury our bones.
Room in the black
For the babe to cry –

For the striped leaves to prod
And relax in the air –
For the long bubble of amethyst
To push from the grass
All bare, all bare

And a green March sun
To give the glad eye
To that mauve openness.
Room for joy's saffron
At the hub, I cry.

THE GIFT

1

No foothold's firm. I throw myself up
Through the tough marram fruiting like wheat.
Rabbits jackknife in the glades of sand.
Bones and dead feathers avoid my feet.

Storm has hollowed sand
Like a potter's thumbs clay on the wheel.
Under a zigzag moon
Waves like a white sea fly.

Up dunes I scramble, to the ragged rims.

Am I meeting you here, Nil o' the Willow?
Or is it to find again
The witch key, moonwort, for you
Where it grows in the slacks?

– But not now, not now.

There's no door to unlock, no opening
In this January night
To be an end . . .

2

When I first met you, you were
Hollow from your widowing,
Bodily almost absent. Only a blown-about soul
Flamed to a thousand shapes
Or lay weak
In a glaze of pain.

You came with me then, to our Thursday's
Convocation, weekly sabbat
In the small hours. Each was God in turn
With bread and wine on the table.

One time God was a drum

And all night we beat bottle or table top.
Twelve hammering priests, or tinkling, fading out
Minutes at a time, then beginning again . . .

      You talked
Of presents and presence. The nowness of gift.

3

Trivia of the miraculous
Started around our Thursday Agape
Like particles spontaneously created
In a field –

Paul, Hugh, Bob, Vikki . . . Dervishes
Whirled. Once God was a devil –
I spoke for him. He gabbled my pride,
My dominion. All the time
Demonstrated my sanctity, my power.

On my knees I begged the others to stop me.
They would not. I saw him smirk
As my plea entered their books. Nothing for it
But to rush out

      Into a night
Of honest storm, tear my hair at home
And die down to exhaustion.

4

But God was gentle sometimes. Sometimes fun.
For in the sixties, sprouting miracles
Answered a dazzlement of the time.

Cults loomed. A modest fame,
Notoriety, spread like a new drug
Through the veins. Students
Truanted to come to us, from Birmingham,
Cambridge, Wrexham . . . Acid heads
Sobered at our meetings.

5

You were hollow with loss, gold and bright
As a candle flame. You, God, talked
Of presents and presence.
The nowness of gift.

And at least my poems answered. I had been lost
Between two modernisms, the abstraction
Of the ruling class, the clutter
Of the ruled.

                    The arbitrary
Otherness of the human
Beckoned in your words. To give
Poems as a presence, like the bread
Of God's flesh
In the unknowably real, a pebble
Or a seed. The nowness of gift.

Llatai, a love-messenger –

Silver
To meld with your gold, tribute to the moon
In the storm, and the blown footsteps
Like mine now, through this shape-shifting dune.

MEINIR AND RHYS

A Noh Play

Cantref of Llŷn

The scene is in the nineteen-sixties. Nant Gwrtheyrn is now a centre for learning Welsh, a valley under the rocky hills of Yr Eifl, called The Rivals in English; but then it lay derelict, abandoned by the stone-quarrying community that once lived there. The events referred to, however, are told of the early nineteenth century, before the quarries opened.

THE PERSONS

John Roberts – a theological student
Meinir
Rhys

Meinir's part is divided between a dancer and a chorus of two actresses who usually speak separately but sometimes in unison.

Rhys only speaks through John Roberts, i.e., the same actor plays two people at once.

John comes on stage and addresses the audience.

John   Foxes have holes, and the birds of the air have nests;
but the Son of Man hath not where to lay his head.

I am a poor theology student, John Roberts from
Prestatyn. My friends have told me of the deserted valley,
Nant Gwrtheyrn, with its square of derelict houses
overlooking the sea. They came to squat here last
summer, and they never cease telling me how beautiful it
was.

I have always wished to see it.
I love solitary places
Where people once lived.

Only the flavour lingers – what they did and suffered
Opening
Sometimes out of broken stones.

Song

The little blue swallow's away from her home,
Over the grey sea she wanders alone,
But when she comes back again, it will be Spring
I drink a health to the power of her wing.

The little blue swallow's gone from the day
Where winter blows cold on hamlet and way,
Harvest is wasted and bare is the lea –
Little blue swallow, come back to me.

The rock of Yr Eifl is grey and forlorn
And lambs on the hillside die where they're born,
The dogs of the blizzard snap at our heels:
Little blue swallow, bring spring to the fields!

John   I have trudged this ancient land,
                 Sand-dunes older than Christ,
                 Fortifications of Mabinogi gods.

                 At every turn of the road
                 Shaman or saint
                 Holds me with some quirk of light.

                 Clynnog the great church
                 Gathers me like a pilgrim.
                 Silence round sacred wells.

                 Fern in the tumbled walls
                 And thorn hedges
                 Earth-red with winter.

                 To Llanaelhaiarn in the cup of the hills,
                 Under the cairns
                 Of burials older than my people

                 Under Tre'r Ceiri, dry-stone city,
                 Where you hear in the winds of the dead
                 Longhorn bulls herded up scree.

                 I climb the hill road from Llithfaen
                 To the saddle of Yr Eifl.
                 Choughs tumble in the air.

                 There is someone coming. Did I see
                 A girl? She looked lost.
                 I'll walk towards her.

Meinir comes down the 'bridge' onto the stage.

Chorus 1   Where is everyone? I've managed it.
                 I've come back.
                 There's no one about.

John	Who do you want? Last summer Some of my friends Stayed in a squat here. Were you in it?
Chorus 1	Last summer, no, there were no strangers then. It was in empty fields We fell in love – only the two of us.
John	Did you live in this valley? Tell me, What happened here? It's so solitary now. I can hardly believe there were children, Lovers laughing together In the glades of the gorse.
Chorus 2	Lovers? Yes, there were lovers.
John	Why can't I see you properly? You're not hiding But it's as if you're not there And your voice didn't belong to you. I hear you Yet the sound comes from nowhere.
Chorus 1	It's not easy.
John	Is it some oddity of the place – A waywardness of light or stone? What happened here?
Chorus 2	Happened?
Chorus 1	Are you asking for history?
Chorus 2	Do you think places listen?

John   Then there isn't a story?
            Your absence is part
            Of your presence, and always will be?

Chorus 2   There are stories, of course.
            Generations don't live
            In a particular place without them.

Chorus 1   They used to tell a story here
            Of a young man Rhys and Meinir his girl.
            The light of the slow waves sang to them.

Meinir starts to dance.

            The tumbling choughs danced their court.
            On the granite the walking cloud
            Dappled their radiance.

            Their marriage would happen.
            Would happen. And the day was chosen.
            Rhys dressed as a bridegroom, went seeking his bride.

            There was a custom, when the bride saw the
                            bridegroom
            She had to run. She had to hide.
            To be reluctant until he found her.

            There was that bit of wilderness
            Before love domesticated them.
            Stallion and mare, they had to run.

            So she saw Rhys walking like a bridegroom
            Towards her. Father opening the gate,
            Her brothers watching. She seized her moment.

            Like a flying partridge in her shawls,
            In her oakleaf brocaded frock
            She fled. She hid, as the custom was.

69

And Rhys searched for her. Searched for her
All afternoon, into the night.
The unbelievable loss of her –

Past hide and seek, anger, despair.
He never found her, never
Climbed into her wilderness

To kiss and kiss and lead her home
And marry her, as
The custom was. Never, never.

Chorus 2   No one set eyes on her. Save that,
Years later, one of the oaks
Was struck by lightning.

Its hollowness was opened, spooned out
Into the air. A dry skeleton
Of a girl and clinging to it

Fragments, mildewed and grey,
Of an oakleaf brocade.
That was all.

John   No, don't go. Who are you?
It's a story, isn't it?
But you're so moved, so involved in it.

Chorus 1   She comes into the light. Unfastens
Her coat. The soft dress
Is burnished with oakleaves.

Chorus 2   She turns to look at him. Smiles
With a smile of the young leaf
Moist from the bud.

John   Who are you? The girl . . .
Meinir?

70

Chorus 1 & 2 (*as Meinir starts to dance*)

> You call me. Yes, Rhys, I have come.

John   As though she looked through me to someone else –
> Someone I thought I was
> For the moment of her smile . . .

(*speaks as Rhys*)

> When we came looking for you, searching,
> Searching through the Nant
> Calling, calling. Meinir, we shouted, Meinir.
>
> Meinir, we're here, Meinir.
> The game's over.
> The priest's waiting.
>
> Then, you did not answer.
> You were faithless, fickle
> As the mist to your friends that loved you.

Chorus 2   She must have heard you.

Chorus 1   She'd run first to the hayricks. Then, crouching
> Down, she thought they'd seen her.
> Apparently, it wasn't a game.

Chorus 2   But it was, wasn't it? I knew it was.

Chorus 1   If it was hide and seek, why did she cling
> So desperately
> To not being found?
>
> She left her nest in the hay.
> It wasn't wilderness enough.
> People could see her.

Chorus 2   I ran to a tree. I climbed into it.

John (as Rhys)

           Not just any tree. It was the oak we played in
                as children,
           Me an orphan, you
           The little girl from the next-door farm.

Chorus 2   Sister and brother. Sister and brother.

Chorus 1   Two children alone under the huge hills.

Chorus 2   Where the fern hung its wings to dry.

Rhys   It cut you if you pulled it. Do you remember?

Chorus 1   And crouching down to find whinberries . . .

Chorus 2   Blackberries you had to reach for –

Chorus 1   I tore my dress. I was smacked for that.

Rhys   We made javelins from elder. The long
           First-year shoots
           Straight and sappy. You could aim them.

Chorus 2   The big pollarded oak, with its room halfway up.

Rhys   Yes, that's where you hid.

Chorus 1   Where they'd cut the trunk, all round
           Like a basket-maker
           It threw up spokes. Long branches to weave with.

Chorus 2   As little children

Rhys   We'd climb up there.

Chorus 1   It was our tree house. Where we talked.

They watch Meinir as she dances their childhood.

Rhys   Why are you lying, Meinir?

The dance stops.

Rhys   You know I was waiting in Clynnog church.
             I did not seek you out,
             Tip the latch on your gate.

             It was not me you saw outside your father's
             To take you to Clynnog.
             That wasn't the custom.

             It was the bridal party you ran from,
             Not me.
             I was left at the church door.

             O later, yes, I came back white and shaken
             To the Nant.
             Days, days, I searched for you then.

Chorus 2   You were marrying me. What's it matter?

Chorus 1   I had to claim my wilderness.
             You were coming.
             I was supposed to run.

Rhys   No, you were coming to me.
             Coming to Clynnog
             With the bridal party . . .

Your wilderness. Your wild flight.
Was it wilderness
To climb into our oaktree?

That secret room of ours,
Where you knew only I
Had the key, hidden by great branches.

Chorus 2   You'd know the secret.

Chorus 1   It was our tree.

Chorus 2   You'd come to me.

Chorus 1   I knew you'd find me.

Rhys   I wasn't supposed to find you.
            I was in the church,
            Waiting, waiting. Remember?

            You were coming to me
            To be my grown-up bride
            Not a child in a tree.

Chorus 2   I've forgotten what happened, that's all.

Chorus 1   My foot knew how to climb,
            Even in a bride's long skirt
            My foot reached for the toe-holds.

Rhys   We'd not been up that oaktree
            Since we were nine or ten.
            What happened then?

Chorus 1   I was hurrying. They might have seen me.
            I had to wait for you
            In the room. Our secret room.

74

Chorus 2   But in those years

Chorus 1   From childhood to marriage

Chorus 2   The heartwood had gone.

Chorus 1   It was hollow. As I trod into it
            In the hasty triumph
            Of climbing into it –

Chorus 2   Foot trod on a remembered floor
            And there was no floor.
            Only a blackness.

Chorus 1   Pain and the dark.

Meinyr begins to dance dreamily of the pain she felt.

Rhys   Did you know we were calling you?

Chorus 2   Did I hear?

Chorus 1   Did I look out and see you?

Chorus 2   Did I smell your fright, your despair?

Chorus 1   The tree knew these things, and it told me
            In its cunning ways, the rind
            Of the tree still alive round me.

            Tree knew in its knotted branches
            It had your imprint.
            You were a grub tunnelling its wood.

            Tree heard you, as it heard thrushes,
            Owls, cuckoos.
            Tree tasted your despair like leafmould.

Rhys   Did you find childhood then?

Chorus 1   No. Not childhood. Pain. Darkness.

Chorus 2   But in that pain I took woodstuff of the tree,
            I put on leaf,
            Curled through the downy bud.

            I gathered myself. I felt my white bones
            Creep from the meat.
            It is not easy, dying down.

            Not easy, to let flesh go
            And still be gathered
            In a bride's watchfulness.

Rhys   You – a bride? Not a child?

Chorus 1   I think I have learnt my bridehood,
            Slowly, out of the oak womb,
            Out of the flooding sap.

            How to be a bride in the grey absence
            Of heartwood.
            I think I have learnt it.

Rhys   And when the lightning struck?

Chorus 2   I don't remember.

Rhys   They found you. Found your bones.

Chorus 1   Yes.

Chorus 2   Yes.

Chorus 1   There were new things I had to learn
            To find my bridehood in
            The open world. To be like breeze.

            To be snow, or rain. To be sunlight
            As it fingers the wet leaf.
            To rest in the coigns of the air.

Chorus 2   And to wait for my lover –

Chorus 1   Bridegroom I had to realise
            In the intensity of waiting.
            Bridegroom I call in you.

Meinir dances. She circles round Rhys, eventually drawing him out into the darkness.

PROGRAMME NOTE

Two of these pieces, 'Old Man Planting Crocus' for Maia, and the Noh play, 'Meinir and Rhys', for Dymphna Darcy to dance to, were written before the sequence was commissioned by Gwynedd County Council in mid October 1995. They are included in the sequence by courtesy of their dedicatees. The commissioned pieces were written with these two in mind, however. I always knew that the sequence would end with the Noh play.

The old Gwynedd County Council, in its death throes before the Tory reorganization of local government, commissioned me to write a sequence of eight to twelve poems in some way about Gwynedd. Alan Llwyd was commissioned to do the same thing in Welsh. I pointed out that I was not a native of the county, and that my sequence would necessarily reflect the experience of an Anglo-Welsh or English incomer from Clwyd. My sponsor accepted this.

In October 1995 the county contained nine ancient cantrefi or 'hundreds', either complete or in large part, together with the cwmwd of Creiddyn (the area round the Great Orme) from the neighbouring cantref of Rhos. However, the cantref of Dinoding is no longer felt as a unit, and is divided customarily into its two cymydau, Eifionydd and Ardudwy. Also, the ecclesiastical maenol of Bangor was generally separated from the rest of the cantref of Arfon. This makes a total of twelve divisions, and my scheme was to write a poem for each.

I call the sequence 'A Gwynedd Symphony' to draw attention to its overall unity. It has less structural resemblance to a classical symphony than my last book, *All Hallows*, but I was clearly conscious as I wrote it of a basic four-movement format. Each movement is made up of two shorter pieces followed by a longer one; and each movement has both a certain symphonic coherence in itself and develops the common themes of the sequence in one particular direction. The very first piece, 'Ferns by Llyn Clyd,' departs most from this scheme because it serves to introduce the whole work, not just its own movement.

A Gwynedd Symphony will only really be seen properly in the context of its fellows – *Castles* and *All Hallows*. Together they form a Commoedia.

Castles is largely an Inferno, a hell's eye vision based on the extent we keep faith or not – and largely not. It is about exploitation, cruelty, alienation, fear, suffering, betrayal and the vanity of human endeavour . . . And perhaps sometimes, something else, the ambiguity of suffering, of the Cross, as not simply hellish but a sign of paradise in our midst. *All Hallows* (as the title implies) is a Purgatorio, about hope and about the two great sins against hope, presumption and despair. Both poems are tragic, symphonic attempts at epic scale without a consistency of epic narrative. They are about individuals, certainly, including me; but they are also an epic vision of Wales and a tragic vision of mankind.

You can have tragedies based on keeping or not keeping faith – the *Agamemnon, Troilus, Macbeth, King Lear*, as you can based on hope – *Prometheus, Oedipus at Colonus, Dr Faustus, Romeo and Juliet*, even (in a strange, inverted kind of way) *Hamlet* and *Mother Courage*. But of course love, the third and greatest virtue of all, the defining virtue of paradise, is also a subject of tragedy – *Antigone, The Women of Troy*, Cordelia, I suppose even *Othello* and *The Winter's Tale*.

So this last of the three poems in my tragic Commoedia, *A Gwynedd Symphony*, is a Paradiso, in the sense that it is about love and the claims of love.

> Man is in love, and loves what vanishes.
> What is there more to say?

Except that love waylays us when we least expect. And in a sense we can vanish but love does not.

12th January, 1996

ADDITIONAL NOTES

Ferns by Llyn Clyd
p. 10. Silurian putsch. The first land plants appeared in the Silurian epoch. The rocks of Snowdonia are actually much older – Cambrian or Ordovician.

Winter at Llanddwyn
For the story of Dwynwen and Maelon and other folklore see *Chwedlau Gwerin Cymru / Welsh Folk Tales* by Robin Gwyndaf (National Museum of Wales, 1992), p. 37. Dwynwen's three wishes were first that Maelon be unfrozen; second that God would answer her intercessions on behalf of true lovers; and third that she should never again wish to be married.
    p. 17. The green room – the actors' common room in a theatre – in the Noh theatre opened onto the playing area and contained a large mirror where the actor-dancers checked their make-up and settled themselves before a performance. (See also the following poem, p. 3.)

The Rhiwledyn Mass of Blessed William Dai
See *Sir William Dai: A Life of the Venerable William Davies, Catholic Martyr* by Patrick J. Crean (Catholic Truth Society, 1985). For obvious historical reasons I have used the Tridentine liturgy in this poem, but I imply no judgement, one way or the other, on the changes introduced since Vatican II.
    p. 18. In that liturgy, when the priest entered the church to say mass, he stopped before the steps to the altar and recited 'Introibo ad altare Dei' –'I will go in unto the altar of God, to God who gives joy to my youth' – and then Psalm 42 (43 in the Anglican numbering): 'Judge me, God, and plead my cause.'
    p. 23. William (Gwilym) Dai's grandfather was a famous *telynor* (harper).
    p. 23. Welsh bardic harp music, extinct save for one undeciphered MS, relied on a patterned alternation of chords on two harmonic centres, the *cyweirdant* (key-note or tuning string) and the *tyniad* (pulling out), which apparently varied according to the tuning. There were conventionally twenty-four 'measures' or patterns of such alternation to match the twenty-four metres of bardic poetry. *Caniad* (lit. a singing) and *gosteg* (usually translated 'prelude' but lit. a silencing) were large-scale compositions of this music. The ways the strings were plucked were also crucially important and systematized.
    p. 24. The Irish poet gave his poem to a *reacaire* who performed it in the

hall of the king or lord; the Welsh poet's equivalent reciter was called an *atceiniad*. A *rhapsode* was a performer in ancient Greece who recited the Homeric epics. *Cynghanedd* ('harmony') is the complex cross-alliteration and rhyming of Welsh bardic poetry.

Pilgrimage

p. 30. The first section imitates a Spanish *vilancico*:

> Tres morillas me enamoran
> en Jaén:
> Axa y Fátima y Marién.

> Tres morillas tan garridas
> iban a coger olivas,
> y hallábanse cogidas
> en Jaén:
> Axa y Fátima y Marién. &c.

p. 33. Bala is on the shores of Llyn Tegid, where the hag Ceridwen lived. She determined to give her son Afagddu the gift of inspiration: her cauldron was to boil for a year and a day to prepare it. Gwion Bach – little Gwion – was set to watch while she gathered the necessary herbs. One day three drops flew out of the cauldron and scalded Gwion Bach's hand. He put his hand in his mouth and immediately understood that Ceridwen would try and kill him. He ran from her, changing into a hare. She pursued as a greyhound. He became a fish, she an otter. Then a bird and she a hawk. Finally he hid as a grain of wheat in a barn; but she as a black, tall-crested hen scratched in the barn and swallowed him. Nine months later she gave birth to a marvellous child, the poet Taliesin.

The Bulls

The story of the fairy cow given to a farmer and then taken back to an under-lake Otherworld is told of several Welsh lakes: this one is Llyn Barfog behind Aberdyfi. See *Chwedlau Gwerin Cymru / Welsh Folk Tales*, p. 60, where the fairy's cattle-calling verse is given. In the last section I have adapted it to the bulls of sovereignty named in the Welsh Triads. Lesley and I went to Buen in Telemark, southern Norway, where an old woman lived until the fifties who every morning sang to the cows in her care. Agnes Buen, herself a traditional singer, played us a recording of the old lady's song. It sounded altogether weird and prehistoric.

p. 55. After the English killed Llywelyn ap Gruffydd, the last independent Welsh ruler, at Cilmeri in 1282, his brother Dafydd proclaimed himself Prince. He was taken near the castle of Bere, Castell y Bere in Merioneth, and barbarously slaughtered.

The Gift

p. 61. Our Thursday's convocation. I saw the film 'Easy Rider' in 1969. It concerned drug smugglers travelling on motor-bikes to the Mardi-Gras in New Orleans; but it was more like a sacred progress, a journey of the Magi, than a thriller. The dialogue (what one could hear of it) seemed both cryptic and evasive. After years of living in an increasingly secular culture – and never more so than when it tried to be pious – this seemed genuinely religious behaviour; and it was reflected in the faces of many students I knew.

I went to see some of them and told them about my experience of the film and that I wanted to learn more. I proposed that we should meet at my house that Thursday night. I said I would supply a loaf of bread and a bottle of wine, the traditional fare of religious communion. I suggested that one of our company should be God for the evening and conduct the meeting as he or she thought best.

These meetings of God Soc went on for about a year and sometimes I was worried that they might take off and become a new religion. One of my colleagues reported me to the College registrar as a drug pusher! But I never used drugs and was more or less intolerant of their presence. Drugs in the sixties were hardly ever an end in themselves. The aim was to clear away falsehood and find spiritual reality.

Meinir and Rhys

For the legend of Meinir and Rhys, see *Chwedlau Gwerin Cymru / Welsh Folk Tales*, p. 39.